**THE MISSING *PEACE*…TO LIVING A LIFE OF PURPOSE**

**Cary A. Knier Johannes, Psy.D.**

Copyright © 2015 by Peace Journeys, Cary Knier Johannes

All rights reserved. No part of this book may be reproduced by any mechanical, photographic, or electronic process, or in the form of a phonographic recording; nor may it be stored in a retrieval system, transmitted, or otherwise be copied for public or private use--other than for "fair use" as brief quotations embodied in articles and reviews--without prior written consent of the publisher.

ISBN-13: 978-0692439494 (Peace Journeys)

**To my loving Creator and supportive family.**

**Tony, Addison and Elise, you give my life purpose every day.**

**Contents**

| | |
|---|---|
| **Chapter 1** | 7 |
| **Chapter 2** | 11 |
| **Chapter 3** | 17 |
| **Chapter 4** | 27 |
| **Chapter 5** | 31 |
| **Notes** | 41 |

# CHAPTER ONE
## *Raising Your Spirit from Infancy to Adulthood*

A seed planted in rich soil is full of life and possibilities. If the seed is nurtured—receives the right nutrients from the rich soil, gets the proper light and is watered—it thrives. The seed doesn't try to make this happen. It doesn't hold its breath and with all its might say, "Grow! Grow!" No, it happens on its own. God takes care of the details.

An infant is a lot like that seed. He doesn't think about growing. He doesn't hold his breath and push himself to grow. He doesn't think, *Will I grow? Will I become an adult? Will I get hair and teeth?* No, infants just *are*. They don't try to make growth happen. It just *does*. God, with caregivers' help, takes care of the details.

Infants are, perhaps, the most spiritual beings. They are conceived and born of the essence of God. They arrive on earth to greet us with God's love. Have you ever observed newborn babies? They move and cry reflexively. They don't think about the motions. They just do them. They are present in the moment without thinking about what happened yesterday or worrying about what will happen tomorrow. If they are hungry, they cry. If they are wet, they cry. They gaze at their parents' faces intently. They give their undivided attention to the moment and take in everything around them—positive or negative.

If, like the seed, an infant is surrounded by love and has his needs met, he will thrive. If, on the other hand, he is surrounded by toxic air and pollutants he will not develop to his full potential. In extremely toxic situations infants may die. Infants absorb the air around them like a sponge. They soak in emotions—healthy and toxic ones. They don't think about it, they just do. Adults may not express these negative emotions, but if they carry them inside infants will absorb them into their bodies. People may not think of infants as spiritual beings, but they are perhaps the most spiritual because they don't have incessant "mind chatter" that interferes with their "being". That is, their thoughts do not interfere with who they are.

We can learn a lot from an infant's presence and undivided attention to help us remember who we are. We are spiritual beings having a human experience. Let me repeat that, we are *spiritual beings* having a *human experience.* We are born from a place of spiritual connection with God. We experience this presence and love in infancy, but somewhere along the way, as we develop, we forget our spirit and think that we are merely humans. We, my friends, are so much more! We come from God—no, we are a part of God. The Divine gives us the opportunity to experience life on earth as humans. It is time for us to wake up and remember who we are, where we come from, and how we can return to our essence while we are here on earth.

I invite you to take this journey of spiritual awakening and remembering. It is a journey of growth and change to know God more intimately. It is a personal quest for the sacred.

## **Spirituality**

This journey is not based on the dogma of one particular religion, but on the ideas and practices of various religions. This journey is more about spirituality and the personal connection you develop with God.

No one definition seems to encapsulate all of spirituality for it is a culmination of many different views. Spirituality is an attempt to give our lives meaning and context. It is a belief in a power operating in the universe that is greater than oneself, a sense of interconnectedness with all living creatures, and an awareness of the purpose and meaning of life and the development of personal values. It is a journey to know God--the Creator--the Divine--that which is bigger than all of us. *Spirituality is an attempt to find the sacred in ordinary moments.*

God is ever-present and stable, but still speaking. We are the ones changing and evolving. We feel a void-- an emptiness inside. We don't know how to feel better or how to feel whole so we turn to worldly "stuff". We buy more electronic devices, bigger houses, spend more time on social media, and consume more food, alcohol, and drugs. We recognize we are not content and attempt to fill this void with these artificial fillers, and yet, nothing satisfies our yearning. We long for the "real deal"—physically and spiritually.

We are on the cusp of change. We are slowly waking up, little by little, to this moment. We are becoming more aware of this dis-ease and starting to recognize what we need to feel nourished. We are attempting to become more intimate with God, the sacred. More of us are remembering who we are. We are discovering that the missing "peace" in our lives is the connection with God.

What if we can awaken sooner? What if it doesn't have to take a crisis or a health scare to wake us from this earthly slumber? What if we can stay awake to the present moment? What if we can awaken sooner so our children never have to fall asleep and forget they are spiritual beings?

Before you can "raise" and nurture your spirit, you will review how infants develop and "lose" their spiritual identity, explore where you are on your own personal journey of wholeness, identify where you would like to be, and learn sacred practices to get there. This book is a tool or workbook to be used along your journey. Feel free to highlight, underline, draw diagrams, or write notes in the margins to help you understand the concepts. It is recommended that you get a notebook or journal to use as a companion for the exercises in this book. You are more likely to complete your goals if you write them down. It is also helpful to look back at a journal and review your journey. Take as much time as you need for each exercise. This book can also be used in conjunction with individual spiritual coaching. If you would like more information about private coaching, please visit www.peace-journeys.com.

Let us journey together towards wholeness.

"Awake, O sleeper! Rise from the dead, and Christ will shine on you!" (The Bible, Ephesians 5:14)

## CHAPTER TWO
## *Human Development*

**Cognitive and physical development in infancy**

In exploring your spiritual journey, it is helpful to understand the process of human development. First, you will review cognitive and physical development and then you will learn about spiritual development according to James Fowler.

During pregnancy, a fetus starts absorbing emotions, events, and words of people around him. He continues to absorb and learn new things during the first year of life. It is amazing to observe all the developmental milestones infants accomplish their first year! They learn how to drink, eat, smile, coo, babble, talk, roll, sit, crawl, walk, and to express emotions. They take everything in, forgetting spirit and evolving more and more into human.

In the first year of life an infant's presence is similar to an animal's presence. The animal exists but does not think about its existence. It does what it needs to in the moment to survive. It does not worry about tomorrow or next week. It lives by instinct.

If you have a pet you understand this concept. You feel its full attention and presence of spirit when it sits next to you or sprawls on your lap. It sits and allows you to pet it. If you give it your full attention, you can feel the animal's energy. You feel connected--your spirit connecting to its spirit.

Have you ever held a baby close to you as she was sleeping? Did you notice her belly rise and fall as you cradled her? Did you just sit and notice? You may have even felt a tingling sensation throughout your body as you sat, fully present and aware of the beauty of *this* moment. You felt connected.

In the second year of life a shift in infant development occurs. Infants begin to develop a sense of "self". The earliest is the "I self"—awareness that the self is *separate* from the surrounding world and can control its thoughts and actions. They can recognize their own actions cause objects and people to react in predictable ways. (1) A familiar example is when the child drops a toy and an adult picks it up and gives it to the child—over and over and over. Another example is when a child smiles at someone, expecting it to be reciprocated.

The second aspect of the self is the "me-self"—a sense of self as an object of knowledge and evaluation. These are all the qualities that make the self unique--individual physical characteristics, possessions, attitudes, beliefs, personality traits. The child becomes aware of the self's features.

In one study, 9-24 month olds were placed in front of a mirror. Each mother was asked to rub red dye on her baby's nose. When each child looked at his image in the mirror, the younger ones touched the mirror as if the red mark had nothing to do with himself but was on the mirror. By 15 months, the toddlers rubbed their own noses. They were aware of their appearance. (2)

By age 2 almost all children recognize themselves in photos and use their name or personal pronoun (I or me) to refer to themselves. Self-awareness becomes the main part of children's emotional and social lives. Self-conscious emotions emerge which is evident when toddlers show bashfulness and embarrassment. This leads to efforts to understand another's perspectives. The first signs of empathy, which is the ability to understand another's emotional state and feel with that person, evolve. At this age, children may try to comfort others when they are crying by using a hug, doll or reassuring comment. (3)

It seems as the "me-self" develops, the "spirit-self" diminishes. Though toddlers are still present in the moment, fully engaged in one activity, their sense of connectedness with spirit fades as the ego emerges and bonds with other humans.

It is difficult to know exactly what happens as toddlers develop or what they really know about spirit because they do not have the language skills to communicate in a way we would understand, nor do they have the cognitive capacity to explain it to us. We can only speculate that as a child develops, she begins to forget her journey from spirit to human. She relates more to humans in her life than to "spirit". If the spirit is not nourished and remembered, its connection fades.

This theme is present in the popular series, *Chronicles of Narnia,* by C.S. Lewis. A young girl, Lucy, and her three older siblings were sent to live in rural England to protect them from the war-torn London. The children tried to find ways to entertain themselves during these long, lonely days. They played hide-and-seek in the large mansion where they stayed. Lucy hid in a large chest and discovered that it led to a magical place called Narnia. There, the four children were kings and queens. The older children did not believe Lucy, but she rediscovered who they really were. She led them to their true selves. She was connected to her true essence. With her persistence, her siblings also rediscovered their true essence. Children are more perceptive to the Spirit, and if are open to them, we can become more perceptive also. Children can remind us of our Divine essence.

## Fowler's Stages of Faith Development

In addition to reviewing cognitive and physical development, it is essential to explore human faith development. A number of people have studied faith development and created theories of development. One of the most widely recognized theories of faith development was proposed by Professor James W. Fowler, a developmental psychologist at Candler School of Theology, in his book *Stages of Faith*. He proposed stages of faith/spiritual development across the life span. (4)

Fowler defines faith as an activity of trusting, committing, and relating to the world based on a set of assumptions of how one relates to others and to the world.

## Fowler's stages

**Stage 0** – *"Primal or Undifferentiated"* faith (birth to 2 years) is characterized by an early learning of the safety of an infant's environment. If consistent nurture is experienced, a child will develop a sense of trust and safety about the universe and the divine. Conversely, negative experiences will cause a child to develop distrust with the universe and the divine.

**Stage 1** – *"Intuitive-Projective"* faith (three to seven years) is characterized by the unconscious, and fluid thought patterns. Religion is learned mainly through experiences, stories, and the people in the child's life.

**Stage 2** – *"Mythic-Literal"* faith (seven to eleven years) is characterized by having a strong belief in fairness and justice. A child's ideas of deities almost always have human qualities and characteristics. Metaphors are often misunderstood and are taken literally.

**Stage 3** – *"Synthetic-Conventional"* faith (twelve years to adulthood) is characterized by the development of a personal identity and conformity to religious authority. A person may not question his beliefs at this stage.

**Stage 4** – *"Individuative-Reflective"* faith (usually mid-twenties to late thirties) is characterized by angst and struggle. A person takes personal responsibility for his or her beliefs and feelings, and may question these beliefs.

**Stage 5** – *"Conjunctive"* faith (usually mid-life) is characterized by a complex understanding of faith and "truth" that may not be explained by one statement or set of beliefs. A person may resolve conflicts about faith through this understanding of a multidimensional approach.

**Stage 6** – *"Universalizing"* faith, or what some might call "enlightenment" (may be mid-life, but not in all individuals) is characterized by a view of a universal community. A person in this stage treats any person with compassion as he or she views people from a universal community of love and justice.

Now that we have reviewed cognitive, physical, and spiritual development, it is time to discover where you are on your spiritual journey. You will explore where you are now, where you would like to be, and learn techniques to move closer to wholeness. The journey for the missing "peace" is a journey of remembering and capturing more sacred moments in our ordinary days. It is a daily practice of remembering God and being fully awake to the moment.

# CHAPTER THREE
## *Where are you now?*

Before we begin a road trip and find directions to our destination, we need to know where we are now. MapQuest, the infamous website for providing directions, requests Point A, your starting location, when you are planning a trip.

Since you are planning a spiritual journey, reflect on your Point A. So, where are you now? How is your spirit? Are you nourishing it? Huge, open-ended questions, right? You might think, *I don't know. How do I answer that??*

It is essential to do some self-exploration as you begin your journey to discovering your missing peace. Finding peace means finding balance in life. With balance comes wellness. On the journey for spiritual wellness, you first need to understand the definition of wellness.

According to the National Wellness Institute *wellness is an active process through which people become aware of, and make choices toward, a more successful existence. (5)*

By applying the Eight Dimensional Model, a person becomes aware of the interconnectedness of each dimension and how they contribute to healthy living. (6)

Below is a summary of the eight dimensions of wellness.

- **Emotional**: Coping effectively with life and creating satisfying relationships
- **Financial**: Satisfaction with current and future financial situations
- **Social**: Developing a sense of connection, belonging, and a well-developed support system
- **Spiritual**: Expanding our sense of purpose and meaning in life
- **Occupational**: Personal satisfaction and enrichment derived from one's work

- **Physical**: Recognizing the need for physical activity, diet, sleep, and nutrition
- **Intellectual**: Recognizing creative abilities and finding ways to expand knowledge and skills
- **Environmental**: Good health by occupying pleasant, stimulating environments that support well-being

Spirituality plays a much larger role in your well-being than the other seven dimensions. It is the core of your wellness. I truly believe that when you make spirituality your priority, the other areas will be easier to balance. It will not make you immune to pain or suffering—there are plenty of examples in the Bible that show us otherwise—but it can make you better equipped to face the pain and suffering when you put God at the center of your life. Finding meaning/purpose in life and in your circumstances will help you find peace. And you find purpose when you connect with God and when you serve others on earth.

## Spirituality and Health

Balance and wellness is part of this journey. Try this exercise. Copy the following phrase with your non-dominant hand:

> *"Our deepest fear is not that we are inadequate. Our deepest fear is that we are powerful beyond measure. It is our light, not our darkness, that most frightens us." ~Marianne Williamson*

When you are finished, ask yourself, what was this like for me? Did it take longer than I expected? Was it frustrating? Was it painful? What else did you notice?

More than likely, you can complete the task, but it is more difficult, takes more time, and is of poor quality. That is the same with wellness. If you do not take care of yourself-- do not nurture your spirit-- you will get some things done, but it will be more frustrating, take longer, and will not be your best quality.

Just as your body needs physical exercise every day, so does your spirit. Your spirit is like a muscle and it needs to be stretched daily for it to grow stronger. When you feed and nourish your spirit, you are nurturing that very part of you that makes you, you. It is the essence of who you really are. It is deeper than your body, more than your thoughts and desires. It is the core of your being that brought you into being.

This essence is like a glowing candle. With more practice and daily nourishment, its flame glows brighter. If forgotten, it grows dimmer until the flame is almost extinguished.

This spark can be most evident at birth and death. When a baby is born, the spark is evident as you feel the energy surrounding this healthy infant. The squirming, the crying, the breathing, the new life all make this flame glow brightly. This was evident at the birth of both of my daughters.

At someone's death, the energy slows as the heart rate and breathing slow, the light in the eyes is gone, the movement stops. This was most clear to me when my grandfather, at 99, was living his last days of life on earth. His body lied in the bed, his chest was rising and falling with uneven breaths, his mouth was open, and his eyes were closed. He did not respond to anything. His body was living, but the essence of who he was, was no longer present. His flame was dim and his spirit was moving on.

Is your flame glowing brightly for others to witness or is it a dim shadow of what could be? Although spirituality and religion may not cure an illness, growing research suggests they can have a positive effect on your health.

Nurturing your spirit:

- ➢ Improves coping skills and social support
- ➢ Fosters feelings of optimism and hope
- ➢ Promotes healthy behavior
- ➢ Reduces feelings of depression and anxiety
- ➢ Encourages a sense of relaxation
- ➢ Positively influences immune, cardiovascular (heart and blood vessels), hormonal, and nervous systems

Recent studies support these health benefits. (7)

- **Prevent depression.** In a study of postmenopausal women, those who reported attending religious services were 56 percent more likely to view life positively and 27 percent less likely to have symptoms of depression than women who did not attend services. (

- **Boost mental health.** Comparing 160 people from different faiths -- Protestants, Catholics, Jews, Muslims and Buddhists -- researchers found that increased religious spirituality was significantly linked to better mental health. Being religious appears to decrease people's sense of self in a positive way, leaving them to feel more connected with the world.

- **Buffer against daily stress.** Everyday religious experiences help people better cope with everyday stress. Being religious seems to protect against the negative impact of daily stressors. It is unclear how spiritual/religious involvement supports health. Some experts say belief in a loving God may directly influence health. Others suggest that spirituality or religious involvement promotes healthier habits, a positive outlook, altruism, better coping strategies in the face of adverse health events, and increased social support through group participation.

## Self-exploration

Another part of this journey to know God more intimately is to know yourself more intimately through self-exploration. Please take some prayerful time to complete the following questions.

**Strengths:** List 5 things you do well that build and maintain your spiritual life (routines, habits, rituals, activities)

1.
2.
3.
4.
5.

- What gives your life meaning?
- What do you value most?
- What helps you feel closer to God?
- What helps you reconnect with your spirit?
- What gives you peace?
- When do you feel balanced and healthy?

➢ What is your daily schedule? How much time do you devote to sacred rituals, such as prayer, meditation, personal reflection or reading sacred texts?

➢ Describe your spiritual journey thus far.

Are you having difficulty answering these open-ended questions? Complete the following inventory to give you more insight about your spiritual life.

# Spiritual Wellness Inventory

**Answer the following by using this scale:**
**2=Almost always  1=Sometimes/occasionally  0=Very seldom/never**

1.___ I feel fully present in each moment.

2.___ I experience a sense of awe and wonder in ordinary moments.

3.___ I appreciate the natural forces that exist in the universe, even if I can't understand them.

4.___ I am willing to forgive myself and others.

5.___ My personal values direct my daily actions.

6.___ My spiritual beliefs and values give me direction when I am frustrated or hurt.

7.___ I participate in regular spiritual activities with people who share my beliefs.

8.___ Rituals, such as prayer, meditation, and/or quiet personal reflection, are important in my life.

9.___ Life is meaningful for me.

10.___ I feel I have a purpose in life.

11.___ I am understanding of others' beliefs.

12.___ I try to learn about others' beliefs and values, especially those different than my own.

13.\_\_\_ I continually explore my personal beliefs, values and priorities.

14.\_\_\_ I am able to speak comfortably about my personal values and beliefs.

15.\_\_\_ I have a strong sense of optimism, and use my thoughts and attitudes in productive ways.

16.\_\_\_ Even when situations seem hopeless, I have faith they can change for the better.

**Scoring your inventory**

Add your total points to find your score.

**0-10** Spirituality is not a significant part of your current life. Many options are available to nurture that part of your life.

**11-22** Spirituality is an evolving part of your life, but you could do a few more things to develop it and nurture it.

**23-32** Spirituality is a significant part of your current life and you are doing many things to nurture it.

Did your score surprise you? Are you satisfied with the level of spirituality in your life? If yes, great—continue to do what you are doing. If not, do not worry, you will learn plenty of ways to nurture your spirit. Be patient and kind to yourself as you journey onward. Before you move forward, be grateful for where you are now. Focus on your strengths and build on those as you move closer to God.

# CHAPTER FOUR
## *Where would you like to be?*

When you plan a road trip, MapQuest also requests Point B, your destination. Now that you have identified Point A on your spiritual journey, it is time to consider Point B. Where would you like to be?

### **Stages of Change**

Do you need to make any changes? If so, are you ready to take the first steps to make these changes? The **Transtheoretical model** of behavior change, or stages of change, assesses an individual's readiness to act on a new healthier behavior. This model proposes that change is a process involving progress through a series of 5 stages. (8)

- **Precontemplation** (Not Ready)--People are not intending to take action in the foreseeable future, and may not be aware that their behavior is problematic.
- **Contemplation** (Getting Ready)--People are beginning to recognize that their behavior is problematic, and start to look at the pros and cons of their continued actions.
- **Preparation** (Ready)--People are intending to take action in the immediate future, and may begin taking small steps toward behavior change.
- **Action**--People have taken specific actions in modifying their problem behavior or in acquiring new healthy behaviors.
- **Maintenance**--People have been able to sustain action for a while and are working to prevent relapse.

If you are contemplating change, picture the life you want and how you want to be living. Spend time in quiet reflection and pray for guidance.

## Destination

What is your destination? How do you want to be living? List 3 things you want in your life.

1.

2.

3.

Now look at the list again. I said 3 things you *want*, not 3 things you *don't want*. The problem is that much of the time people spend energy thinking about the things they don't want to happen. You worry and fret over the things you don't like or want, like the crinkles that have suddenly appeared around your eyes, the extra pillow you find around your belly or the anxiety your child experiences at school. You forget to focus on what you do want in life. Life is what you make of it and it can be different, even better, than what it has been.

Some people argue, *If I don't worry, things won't get done* or *If I plan for the worse, I'll be prepared for anything.* On the contrary! Research shows that we waste a lot of time and energy planning escape routes and failure plans before we even set a positive goal and an action plan to achieve that goal. (9)

The key to making any change is to visualize the goal—to clearly picture what it is you do want. Spend some time visualizing your goals. Give yourself time to sit quietly, uninterrupted, and pray. Ask God to guide you as you visualize your life.

Imagine how you want to live your life. Picture how you want to treat yourself and others. Visualize how you want to think, feel, and behave. Make it as real as possible in your mind. Ponder the following questions and write out the answers in a journal.

- What do you think about most?

- What do you want most?

- What will you be doing differently?

- What motivates you to make changes?

- Why do you want these changes?

- What do you find meaningful in life?

- What brings you the most joy?

**Life Purpose Statement**

Using the answers to these questions, write a Life Purpose Statement or Personal Mission. This is a guide for your life. This summarizes your mission in life. It should be something you can use in all situations and through different phases of your life. Keep it concise and brief (3-4 sentences).

After you have a clear picture of that life, write out the details of your thoughts, feelings and behaviors. This detailed account will guide your goal setting process.

**Goals**

Make **SMART** goals. Your goals need to be **s**pecific—make them detailed. They need to be **m**easurable—state them so you can measure your progress. Goals should be **a**ttainable—they should be something you can achieve. They should be **r**ealistic—make sure you have the potential and resources to meet the goals. Goals should be **t**imely—set a deadline so you fulfill the goals. Most importantly, write them down. You are more likely to achieve goals if you record them.

Now that you have clear goals and are ready to take action, continue on your journey to learn ways to achieve your goals and become more intimate with your true essence.

# CHAPTER FIVE
## *How will you get there?*

Have you noticed that your mind is always thinking, thinking, thinking? For most, it is difficult to quiet your thoughts long enough to actually connect with God in an authentic way. Much of the time your connections feel superficial and you crave a deep, intimate connection with your Creator.

Quieting your mind not only helps you connect with the Creator but can also help reduce symptoms of anxiety and depression. Relaxing your minds and bodies can lower blood pressure and the effects of stress.

Many options to quiet your mind are available but the key is to find the right ones for you and to make the time to practice them. Try several of the following practices and notice which ones resonate with you. Remember any of these will work for some people, but they will only be effective if you take the time to *practice* daily.

### **Daily Prayer**

Spending time each day in prayer is essential in building your relationship with God. Some people worry about what to say. They think *I am not a pastor or a religious teacher, my words are not good enough for God.* The words don't matter as much as your intention. As long as you desire to be more intimate with the Holy Spirit, the words will emerge from your heart. Allow time to talk to God and to listen to God.

Some people pray memorized prayers (such as the Lord's Prayer), some pray silently, others pray aloud. Some pray individually while others pray in groups. The details don't matter as much as your intention. This is between you and God. God knows your heart!

## Prayer Beads

Prayer beads are used in many religions and cultures throughout the world. Earliest traces of praying with beads can be found in the ancient Hinduism of India. Many faiths have used them to practice devotion and meditation based on pattern and repetition. You can use a beaded necklace or bracelet, a rosary or make your own prayer beads. These are tools that guide our hearts to God.

Begin by taking the main bead and ask God to be present in your practice. Say something like
*O God be with me today.* Be yourself and invite God into your prayer. You can use a prayer you memorized as a child or make one up.

Move to the next bead. Rest a single bead between your thumb and forefinger. Take a deep breath. Pray.

There is no right way to pray. Some people choose their favorite scripture, or favorite hymn, with each bead a different verse. Some even pray for something new on each bead: "For my neighbor and her cancer" or "For the upcoming medical tests I have" or "Thank you for the flowers blooming". Say your prayers aloud, in silence, or with a group.

## Lectio Divina

Lectio Divina literally means "divine reading." This *holy reading* is a way of praying the words of the Bible. Early Christians used lectio divina as a meditative tool to go deeper with God and these holy texts. (10)

This practice reveals what God is saying to you. Often God may be calling you to quiet your racing thoughts. At other times, God may be calling you to question life, your faith, your values, and your motivations. No matter where this practice seems to lead you, it will always bring you a bit closer to God.

First, read the text slowly and carefully. Choose any text from the Bible, but the shorter the better. Close your eyes and take a deep breath. Focus on what God is saying to you. Read it out loud. Read it silently.

Reflect on the text. Read it several times and pray about the text. Pray that God may open your heart and mind to understanding.

Next rest your mind. Close your eyes, breathe, and listen.

Lastly, note what God is leading you to do. What did the text reveal to you? Write it down and do what you feel called to do.

## **Gratitude Journal**

People who are grateful tend to be happier, healthier and more fulfilled. Being grateful can help people cope with stress and lower heart rate. In tests, people who tried keeping a gratitude journal each night for just one week were happier and less depressed one month, three months and six months later. Scriptures from the Bible teach the importance of gratitude: "Rejoice always, pray continually, give thanks in all circumstances; for this is God's will for you in Christ Jesus." (The Bible, I Thessalonians 5:16-18). Now science shows evidence that gratitude is good for you. People often take things for granted and our brains naturally pay attention to negative events and thoughts. If you want to feel happier and living more meaningful lives, you have to consciously focus on the good things in your lives and get in the habit of being grateful. Remember, it takes at least 3 positive comments to outweigh one negative comment! (11)

At the end of each day, think back over your day and remember three good things that happened. These can be small or big things. Be specific—don't just say 3 general things, such as family, friends, and health. Those things are important, but the goal is to focus on 3 particulars of this day.

Write these specific situations in a special notebook. Write down what and why you are grateful for each situation.

Try doing this for at least 3 weeks to develop the habit. Review your entries at the end of each week, month and year. Notice how you feel after reviewing all that you are grateful for. Also notice if any themes are present and what that means to you.

## Conversations with God

This is another journaling technique that helps you connect with God. It is particularly helpful if you have a lot on your mind and find it difficult to quiet your thoughts.

Adjust your schedule so you have an extended period of time to write. Go to a quiet, relaxing place with a journal or notebook and writing tool. Get comfortable.

Spend a few minutes praying, asking God to be with you and guide you.

Next, write any thoughts that come to your mind. They don't have to make sense or be grammatically correct. Just write. It may be something you have been contemplating--a decision you need to make or emotions you have been feeling. There are no limits to the topics you write. Bring them all to God.

Continue to write until you have no more to say or when you feel a gentle nudge to stop. Then close your eyes and listen. Focus on your breath and listen to the still, quiet voice within.

When you notice these quiet thoughts, write them down. Again, just write. Do not worry about what you are writing. (Some people prefer to listen first and then write these thoughts later.)

Think of these words of wisdom as guidance from your Spirit. This opens the door to hear God's prompting in your life. People often cannot hear God prompting them until they clear the mind chatter. Journaling your thoughts can help clear this internal chatter and open your heart and mind to the Divine inspiration you are seeking. Spend as much or little time in this quiet space as you need.

## **Relaxed Breathing**

Breathing is something you do every day but you rarely think about it. Breathing is automatic but you also have the power to alter it. By taking deeper, slower breaths you can lower your blood pressure and improve circulation. The breath is also referred to as "Ruach", a Hebrew word that translates to "spirit". When you connect to your breath, you connect to Spirit. Here are a couple of breathing exercises to try:

1. Sit upright in a chair, feet flat on the floor. Place one hand on your chest and one on your belly. Inhale and exhale through your nose several times. Notice which hand moves more. The goal is to take deeper breaths so you want the hand on your belly to move more. If the hand on your chest is moving more, try to focus your attention on your belly. Breathe from the belly. If this is too difficult, try lying on your back and allow your belly to rise and fall with each breath. Notice your breath. Start with 10 breaths. Eventually extend the time to 10 minutes of relaxed breathing.

2. Using the same belly breathing as above, focus on slowing the breath down, making it longer and deeper. Make your exhale twice as long as your inhale to make it a more relaxed breath. Sit upright in a chair, feet flat on the floor. Inhale through your nose for a count of 4 and then exhale through your nose for a count of 8. As you exhale, say to yourself, *Relax.* Again, inhale…1, 2, 3, 4….exhale, *Relax*…1, 2, 3, 4, 5, 6, 7, 8. Repeat this for 10 cycles, twice daily.

If counting to 8 is too long for you, try 6 or 7 counts. This is supposed to help you relax so don't make it too difficult!

3. Taking deeper breaths throughout the day is beneficial for your body and your spirit. Take a deep breath whenever you have to wait at a stop light, when you are in line at the store, when you are on hold on the phone, or at the beginning of each hour, on the hour. By getting into this habit of taking deep breaths throughout the day, you will be reducing stress, lowering your blood pressure, and connecting with God.

## **Meditation**

Meditation is a universal practice of calming the mind that has been used for thousands of years. Meditation is a technique for relaxing the mind and attaining a state of awareness. People often find that meditation helps quiet their thoughts and become more attune to Spirit.

Sit or lie in a quiet space. Close your eyes and take a few cleansing breaths in and out through your nostrils.

Let your body breathe naturally and focus your attention on your breath. Do not try to alter it or slow it down—just notice it.

Some people focus on their belly as it rises and falls with each inhale and exhale. Others notice their breath as it enters their nostrils and fills their lungs. Often people rotate their attention to these different areas of breath. The key is to follow your breath as you inhale and continue to follow it as you exhale.

Each breath is like a wave in the ocean. Your breath rises as you inhale, just like the wave rises. As your breath reaches its full capacity, it pauses slightly, just as the wave reaches its fullest height. Your breath then falls as you exhale, just as the wave recedes after it peaks.

Notice your breath as it rises and falls, following it to its conclusion. If meditation is a new practice for you, start with 2-3 minutes of quiet meditation and continue to extend the time so you can meditate for 20-30 minutes in one sitting.

Remember, your thoughts will still try to interrupt your meditation—this is normal! Human brains are meant to think. The key is to notice the thoughts and allow them to fall away, just as the waves fall away in the ocean. Don't get angry at yourself for the thoughts, just let them be like background music in your car. They are there, but don't pay much attention to them. Focus on your breath. Be gentle and kind to yourself as you build your practice.

## Grounding Exercise

This visualization exercise helps quiet your thoughts and be more aware of your body. People spend much time in their minds, thinking about all the projects that need to be finished or wondering what someone else is thinking or judging something they see. People are rarely fully present to notice sensations in their bodies. This exercise trains you to be more focused and aware of your body and the energy inside.

Sit in a quiet place, feet flat on the floor and hands resting on your lap. Take your time with this exercise. Pause at each area of your body before moving to the next. Close your eyes and take several cleansing breaths, breathing from your diaphragm.

Draw your attention to the earth below your feet. Feel the energy from the earth swirling just beneath your feet. Now let that energy enter the bottom of your feet and spread throughout your feet. You might notice a tingling sensation in your feet.

Notice that energy expand as it rises into your ankles, circling your left ankle and then your right ankle. You might feel the vibration of the energy spiral higher around your shins and calves. Let that energy spiral around your legs for a moment.

Now draw your attention to your knees as you feel the energy circle your knee caps. The energy continues to rise up into your thighs. Feel the electricity flow up and down your thighs.

After a moment notice the energy transmitting from your thighs to your hands. Feel the slight pulsing in your fingers. Let that energy spread into your hands. Feel your hands pulsate as if they had tiny heart beats.

The energy is now spreading into your wrists. Feel the energy circle your left wrist. Now feel it circle your right wrist.

Notice the energy as it flows up into your forearms. Feel it flow up and down.

Now notice it hovering around your elbows. Let the energy spiral up around your biceps and then your triceps.

The energy now spreads up into your shoulders. Feel the electricity spread through your shoulder blades.

Now imagine that your head is detached from your body. Let it float up gently, like a balloon. Focus your attention on your body. Let your body breathe as one whole organism. Take a few moments to feel it breathe. Imagine that your pores are opening up and allowing oxygen in through your skin and releasing carbon dioxide out.

After a few moments of body breathing, imagine your head is descending slowly, down, down, down into your belly. Focus your attention on your belly as you breathe in and out. Breathe in and out gently through your nostrils. Feel your belly expand and contract with each breath.

Let your head ascend and land just at the top of your neck, right where it naturally sits. Continue to breathe from your belly.

After a few minutes of relaxed breathing, slowly open your eyes. Continue to focus your attention on your feet, legs, and belly as you become more aware of your external surroundings. Pay attention to the internal sensations while beginning to notice the external surroundings.

When you are fully awake and aware, continue to practice dividing your attention between your bodily sensations and your surroundings. This will train your brain to focus on the present moment and not be aimlessly thinking unproductive thoughts.

This exercise not only increases your brain's ability to focus, but also helps you align with Spirit.

## **Blessings**

Many practices and techniques are available to quiet your mind and connect with Spirit. The techniques are not right or wrong, good or bad. The key is to practice several techniques and discover which ones work best for you. And, most importantly, make the time in your daily life to focus on the present moment and to connect with your true essence, the Spirit of God.

You have come a great distance on this journey for the sacred. You have identified where you started, where you would like to be, and ways to get there. You identified ways to balance your life, bringing you into balance and wholeness by focusing on your relationship with the Divine Spirit. The missing "peace" is the lack of spiritual connectedness to God. To attain this peace, you need only spend more time with God and be fully present in each moment.

Though you have come to the end of this book, your journey is not over. Your journey will continue to grow and change for the rest of your time on earth. You have a choice about the type of journey you will take. Will you choose to journey alone or will you choose to journey in Spirit with God? If you would like to work with a spiritual life coach and to find out more about other services available, please visit www.peace-journeys.com to connect with me.

May you always remember your true essence as a spiritual being! Peace and blessings~

# NOTES

(1) Laura Berk, *Development Through the Lifespan*, Third Edition (New York: Allyn and Bacon, 2004), 195.

(2) Laura Berk, *Development Through the Lifespan*, Third Edition (New York: Allyn and Bacon, 2004), 195.

(3) Laura Berk, *Development Through the Lifespan*, Third Edition (New York: Allyn and Bacon, 2004), 195.

(4) James Fowler, *Stages of Faith The Psychology of Human Development and the Quest for Meaning* (New York: Harper Collins, 1995).

(5) To learn more about wellness go to the National Wellness Institute website, http://www.nationalwellness.org/?page=Six_Dimensions.

(6) You can find more information about the 8 dimensions of wellness at the Substance Abuse and Mental Health Services Administration (SAMHSA) website, http://promoteacceptance.samhsa.gov/10by10/dimensions.aspx.

(7) Check this website for more information: www.johnshopkinshealthalerts.com/alerts/depression_anxiety/Health-Benefits-of-Spirituality_6449-1.html

(8) James Prochaska, Colleen Redding, Kerry Evers, "TheTranstheoretical Model and Stages of Change", *Health Behavior and Health Education Theory, Research, and Practice*, 4TH Edition (San Francisco: Wiley & Sons, 2008), 98. http://fhc.sums.ac.ir/files/salamat/health_education.pdf#page=135

(9) Shawn Achor, *Before Happiness: The 5 Hidden Keys to Achieving Success, Spreading Happiness, and Sustaining Positive Change* (New York: Crown, 2013).

(10) Check the United Church of Christ's website www.ucc.org for more practices

(11) Shawn Achor, *Before Happiness: The 5 Hidden Keys to Achieving Success, Spreading Happiness, and Sustaining Positive Change* (New York: Crown, 2013).

www.ingramcontent.com/pod-product-compliance
Lightning Source LLC
Chambersburg PA
CBHW061347040426
42444CB00011B/3132